# Int

More than a ~
supplement th~
supplements. ~ ...gredients and
formula combinations have become quite
diversified to suit a variety of consumer needs –
they are no longer just taken as insurance to
prevent a vitamin or mineral deficiency. The past
fifty years of medical research has proven that
supplements can also be used to help enhance
your body's structure and function. Supplements
can also be very beneficial as nutritionally
supportive therapy in treating certain illnesses.

The mineral calcium is a classic example of
how supplements can improve the structure of
your body. Calcium is found throughout your
body, but is mainly known for its role in bone
formation and maintenance. Calcium can be
obtained from food, but supplements have been
shown to be more effective in building healthy,
strong bones. Furthermore, it is now well
established that taking calcium supplements
may prevent osteoporosis and can even be used
to halt the progression of the disease. Recent
reports have revealed that essential nutrients,
such as magnesium and vitamin D help calcium
to build and maintain strong bones throughout
your life.

When it comes to maintaining your body's
function, a diversity of new nutritional
supplements have appeared on the market.
Sometimes the discovery of a new use for an
existing essential vitamin or mineral leads to the
formulation of a speciality product, such as
calcium's role in buffering stomach acidity and

supporting nervous system function. Or how zinc, vitamin A, vitamin C and iron can boost your immune system function and help you ward off certain infections and diseases. Then there is the collection of plant (botanical/herbal) supplements. Medical research has discovered a wide variety of uses for botanicals. Some of the popular botanicals include, ginkgo for better memory and circulation, ginseng for energy, and garlic for reducing cholesterol.

This A to Z guide is therefore written to provide you with quick reference information about the most popular ingredients you will find in nutritional supplements. In Section One you will find each supplement listed alphabetically, giving you a brief background of the ingredient and elaborating on its key benefits.

Following the A to Z section is a "Use Summary" section. Here you can find information about which supplements will, for example, promote longevity, help men or benefit women most. Also included are summaries about which supplements medical science has shown will help you prevent or heal ailments such as arthritis, cardiovascular disease, depression, diabetes, fatigue, digestive illnesses, a compromised immune system, memory loss, menopause, sleep disorders, stress, etc.

The final section of this guide is a glossary.

This A to Z guide will truly put you in charge of your health.

# Contents

# Section One:

# A to Z of Nutritional Supplements

Nutritional supplements included in this section:

**A**
Agnus Castus **7**
Aloe Vera **8**
Antioxidants **9**
Arginine **10**
Artichoke Extract **11**
Avena Sativa **12**

**B**
Bee Propolis **13**
Beta-carotene **14**
Biotin **15**
Black Cohosh **16**
Boron **17**

**C**
Calcium **18**
Cat's Claw **19**

Chitosan **20**
Chloride **21**
Chondroitin Sulphate **22**
Chromium **23**
Cod Liver Oil **24**
Co- Enzyme Q10 **25**
Copper **26**
Cranberry **27**

**D**
Devil's Claw **28**
Dong Quai **29**

**E**
Echinacea **30**
Evening Primrose Oil **31**

# CONTENTS

# Agnus Castus

- **Eases PMS discomfort, especially breast tenderness**
- **Regulates female hormone levels**
- **Restores a normal menstrual cycle**
- **Best for premenopausal women**

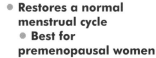

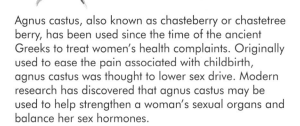

Agnus castus, also known as chasteberry or chastetree berry, has been used since the time of the ancient Greeks to treat women's health complaints. Originally used to ease the pain associated with childbirth, agnus castus was thought to lower sex drive. Modern research has discovered that agnus castus may be used to help strengthen a woman's sexual organs and balance her sex hormones.

**Use:** Agnus castus can be used to relieve menstrual cycle irregularities and PMS complaints. PMS symptoms, such as swollen and tender breasts, are thought to be associated with elevated levels of the hormone prolactin. Therefore, agnus castus' prolactin-lowering effects are thought to play a vital role in restoring normal menstrual cycle and relieving PMS discomfort.

# Aloe Vera

- **Promotes a healthy digestive system** ● **Supports healthy skin**
- **Has soothing and healing properties**

Aloe vera is one of the world's oldest medicinal herbs – it has a history of traditional use going back over 4,000 years. The ancient Egyptians, Franciscan monks and even Alexander the Great were devotees of the botanical. It was rediscovered in the 1930s when doctors found that it soothed radiation burns from X-rays when all other methods failed.

Aloe vera is comprised of more than 200 biologically active constituents, which may help explain the herb's vast repertoire of healing properties. Positive scientific studies on aloe vera have been published for decades; its healing abilities cannot be challenged.

**Use:** Aloe gel is well known for the promotion of healthy skin. Internally, aloe vera is taken to promote a healthy stomach lining and normal digestion. The bitter fraction of the aloe leaf has been used for centuries as a cathartic, stimulating the rhythmic contractions of the intestines, which move digested food on the journey from the stomach to the rectum. This is found in whole leaf aloe products.

# Antioxidants

Antioxidants are essential for overall health and are the ultimate anti-ageing nutrients. They reduce damage to the body's cells from both naturally occurring and introduced chemicals. Specifically, these nutrients have the ability to prevent oxidation and neutralise free radicals – unstable compounds that react with and damage other substances in the body. Clinical studies show that antioxidants work in synergy with each other. To ensure good health, take a number of different types of antioxidants, enabling you to best protect the whole body and all of its complex systems and tissues. Recent studies on centenarians have revealed a clue to their longevity secret – they have higher levels of antioxidants in their body.

For more information on antioxidants please see the entries on:

- Vitamin C
- Vitamin E
- Ginkgo biloba
- Grape Seed Extract
- Beta-carotene

- Free Radicals
- Selenium
- Vitamin A
- Lutein
- Lycopene

# Arginine

- **Promotes wound healing**
- **Supports circulatory system health**
- **Elevates growth hormone levels**
- **Promotes longevity**
- **Creates feelings of well-being**
- **Stimulates immune system function**

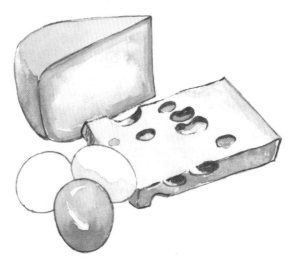

Arginine is classified as a non essential amino acid because the body can make enough for its own needs. Arginine is involved in several metabolic pathways in the body, such as elevating growth hormone levels; creatine manufacture; wound healing; circulatory system health; fertility; sexual performance; and in the detoxification of the metabolic waste product ammonia. Arginine is becoming a popular longevity nutrient due to its ability to increase growth hormone levels and promote a healthy circulatory system.

# Artichoke Extract

- **Increases bile production**
- **Lowers cholesterol levels**
- **Promotes liver health**
- **Supports digestive health**

Artichoke is perhaps best known as an edible vegetable. Artichoke extract is derived from the lower leaves of the artichoke plant. It has been used since early Greek times as both a culinary delight and a healing herb. Artichoke has been the favoured dish of many famous people, including King Henry VIII.

**Use:** As the Greeks discovered, artichoke extract is also a powerful herbal remedy. The benefits of artichoke extract include: healthy bile excretion, promotion of liver health, lowering cholesterol levels and supporting a healthy digestive system.

# Avena Sativa

- **Eases dry, itchy skin**
- **Improves libido**
- **Reduces risk of coronary heart disease**

We all know that avena sativa, better known as oats, are a healthy, nutritious food. Oats are rich in a number of nutrients including calcium, zinc, magnesium, iron and protein. Recently, the U.S. Federal Food and Drug Administration authorised a health claim for whole oats, allowing manufacturers to state that a diet that includes soluble fibres, such as those found in oats, may lead to a reduced risk of coronary heart disease. You may also be interested to know that oat extract products have traditionally been used as aphrodisiacs for men and women.

# Bee Propolis

- **Natural immune protector**
- **Soothes gastrointestinal distress**
- **Heals skin blemishes**

Bee propolis has a long history of use dating back over 2,000 years. Bee propolis is a sticky substance collected by bees from plants, in particular, conifers. Propolis is rich in bioflavonoids (a type of antioxidant) and substances that have been shown to display anti-microbial and anti-inflammatory activity. It has been traditionally used internally to promote natural immunity and gastrointestinal health, in particular to reduce inflammation and heal certain types of ulcers. In addition to possible internal benefits, bee propolis is used in topical products for a variety of healing purposes, as in treating bruises, burns and skin blemishes.

# Beta-carotene

- **Functions as an antioxidant**
- **Promotes healthy eyesight**
- **Improves immune function**
- **May prevent certain types of cancer**
- **May reduce risk of cardiovascular disease**
- **Decreases risk of certain eye disorders**

Beta-carotene, or provitamin A, is an antioxidant produced by plants. It is one of the two forms of vitamin A and as a vitamin A precursor enhances the immune system response. Its vitamin A activity makes it an essential nutrient, with additional semi-essential health functions. In plants, beta-carotene functions as a pigment, which gives carrots their characteristic orange color.

**Use:** The nutrient's antioxidant activity protects the body from metabolic damage, which is important for maintaining proper biological structure and function, and lowering the risk of developing degenerative diseases. Beta-carotene is also considered an alternative way to assure adequate vitamin A status because once in the body, the substance is converted into the vitamin on an as-needed basis.

# Biotin

- **Vitamin B**
- **Essential in energy production**
- **Important for good health**

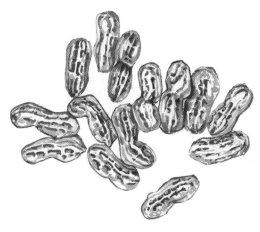

A water-soluble essential vitamin that is a member of the B vitamin group, biotin is involved in new cell growth, glucose formation, fatty acid synthesis, energy production and urea formation. Biotin supplements may delay baldness and grey hair. Biotin deficiency can lead to loss of appetite, anaemia, baldness, high blood sugar, nausea, vomiting, depression, muscular pain, increased serum cholesterol concentration, loss of muscle tone, soreness of the tongue, and a dry, scaly dermatitis.

# Black Cohosh

- **Eases menopausal symptoms**
- **Soothes premenstrual pain**
- **May lower blood pressure**

During the menopause oestrogen levels steadily decrease; at the same time a substance known as luteinizing hormone increases. The increase in luteinizing hormone is believed to cause the hot flushes and other uncomfortable symptoms associated with the menopause. Black cohosh suppresses luteinizing hormone levels, thereby minimising the side effects that excess levels of the hormone can cause.

**Use:** Studies have confirmed that intake of standardised black cohosh reduces other uncomfortable symptoms associated with menopause such as hot flushes, nervousness, anxiety and depression. Black cohosh has also been shown to be effective for relieving premenstrual discomfort and menstrual cramps. Improvements are seen after several weeks to three months of daily use.

# Boron

- **Supports bone health**

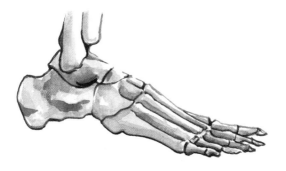

Boron is an essential trace mineral that occurs in the body in small amounts. It has not been established exactly how boron works in the body but it appears to play an important role in bone health, formation and maintenance.

# Calcium

- **Builds strong bones and teeth**
- **Prevents osteoporosis**
- **Normalises blood pressure levels**
- **Regulates heartbeat**
- **Has calming effect on the nervous system**
- **Buffers acidity**
- **Needed to metabolise iron**
- **Aids muscular contractions**

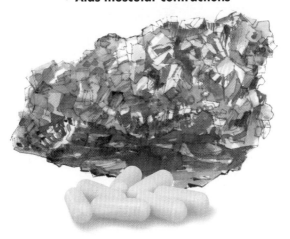

Calcium is the most abundant mineral in the body. It is mainly found in our bones and teeth with small amounts apparent in the blood, muscle and body tissues. Calcium is essential for building strong bones and teeth; preventing bone loss and osteoporosis; and regulating blood pressure. Despite the abundant information showing calcium's importance, especially for women, it remains one of the minerals most likely to be deficient in the diet, making supplementation essential for optimal health.

# Cat's Claw

**Stimulates the immune system**

**Anti-viral**

**May aid in the treatment of a number of degenerative diseases**

Cat's claw (uncaria tomentosa) is an alkaloid-rich plant harvested from woody vines that grow over one hundred feet in length as they attach and wind their way up through the trees of the Peruvian rain forests. The herb gets its common name, cat's claw, from the two curved horns at the base of each leaf. It supports and stimulates the immune system and shows anti-viral acitivity similar to the more well known botanical,echinacea. Used in South America to help maintain overall health.

# Chitosan

**• Reduces cholesterol levels**
**• Can function as a weight loss aid**

Chitosan is a fibrous substance of animal origin.
It is derived from a compound called chitin, found in
the exoskeletons of shellfish such as crabs, lobsters,
and shrimp. Chitosan blocks the absorption of fats
in the digestive system, thereby lowering the amount
of fat and cholesterol that goes into the bloodstream.
It helps maintain healthy cholesterol levels and can
function as a weight loss aid.

As long term or constant use could affect the
take up of the fat soluble vitamins, such as Vitamin A
and E, chitosan should be taken 4 hours after any
vitamin supplements.

# Chloride

- **Promotes normal digestion**
- **Essential for health**

Chloride is important to the body as an anion (a negatively charged molecule) in extracellular fluid (any fluid that is found in the areas of the body outside the cells, such as blood, lymph, and interstitial fluid, or fluid between cells and tissues). Chloride plays a role in both fluid and blood acid-base balance. It is also a component of the stomach's digestive juice secretions, required in the formation of hydrochloric acid. Chloride is also one of the electrolyte minerals, which, along with sodium and potassium, regulates the flow of water between cells and the bloodstream. Chloride promotes normal body function. It maintains the body's water balance and promotes normal digestion function in the stomach.

# Chondroitin Sulphate *(Sulfate)*

- **Supports connective tissue and joint health**
- **Maintains circulatory system health**
- **Eases arthritis discomfort**
- **Improves wound healing**

As we age, our connective tissues can become increasingly worn, causing joint mobility problems and degenerative diseases. Chondroitin sulphate is an important component of the connective tissues that make up our joints. It gives cartilage and ligaments their flexibility and attracts water to these tissues, thereby maintaining proper hydration. Supplementation with chondroitin sulphate has been shown to improve the condition of connective tissues; improve tissue repair and wound healing; treat osteoarthritis by restoring joint function and reducing pain; and cause improvements in circulatory system wellness by increasing structure of the inner lining of blood vessels.

# Chromium

- **Can help in weight management**
- **Helps in the treatment of diabetes**

Chromium is an essential mineral. Its major biological role is as a potentiator of insulin; that is, it helps insulin do its job. It is also important in carbohydrate metabolism. Chromium also functions in the maintenance and metabolism of nucleic acids. Studies report that taking chromium supplements can help in weight management by increasing fat loss and by maintaining or increasing muscle tissue. Other functions of chromium include stabilising blood sugar levels; improving insulin functioning; and helping in the nutritional management of diabetes.

# Cod Liver Oil

- **Maintains joint flexibility**
- **Promotes a healthy heart and circulatory system**
- **Builds healthy bones, skin, hair and nails**

Cod liver oil is rich in omega-3 fatty acids such as EPA and DHA. These two substances are linked with lowering triglycerides (fatty substances in the blood) – thus helping to prevent heart disease – and inhibiting atherosclerosis (hardening of the arteries). Cod liver oil is the ideal supplement for anyone seeking to maintain optimum health.

# Co-enzyme Q10 *(Co Q10)*

- **Reduces oxidative damage**
- **Reduces body fat**
- **Enhances immune system function**
- **Improves athletic performance**
- **Lowers blood pressure**

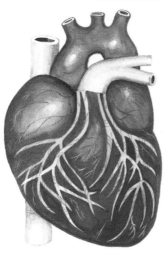

CoQ10 involved in energy production in all cells and functions as an antioxidant. It plays a role in the proper function and maintenance of a healthy heart and circulatory system. Supplemental intakes of CoQ10 have been associated with the following benefits: improved heart function; reduced free radical damage of LDL-cholesterol; lowering of blood pressure; greater reduction of body fat in dieting obese females (than with diet alone); immune system enhancement; improved athletic performance in endurance sports. It also promotes periodontal health and helps reduce gingivitis.

# Copper

- **Important to immune system function**
  - **Keeps blood vessels, nerves and bones healthy**

Copper is an essential mineral needed (along with iron) for the formation of haemoglobin, which carries oxygen in the body. It is present in many enzymes and important in the formation of collagen, melanin synthesis, immune function and energy production. It helps keep blood vessels, nerves and bones healthy. Supplementation ensures adequate dietary copper for maintenance of health.

# Cranberry

- **Maintains bladder and kidney health**
- **Source of vitamin C**

Cranberry has a history of use for combating urinary tract infections. Medical research has recently confirmed that phytonutrients found in cranberries reduce the ability of infectious bacteria to cling to the inner surfaces of the urinary tract and cause infection. Regular consumption of cranberry juice has been associated with reducing urinary tract infections, bladder infections and chronic kidney inflammation.

# Devil's Claw

- **Eases arthritis pain and inflammation**
- **Aids in digestive health**
- **Used to treat gout and rheumatism**
- **Promotes liver, kidney and**

Devil's claw (harpagophytum procumbens), so-named because of its large, claw-shaped fruit, contains phyto-nutrients with varied biological effects. Certain ingredients found in devil's claw have been shown to have anti-inflammatory activity and are considered the most biologically active components of devil's claw. Used for joint pain and inflammation; to stimulate appetite and digestion; as an analgesic and for dyspepsia, gallbladder dysfunction and rheumatism.

# Dong Quai

- **Eases menopausal symptoms**
- **Regulates hormone levels**
- **Improves blood circulation**
- **Relieves PMS symptoms**
- **Has a mild calming effect**
- **Alleviates constipation**

Dong quai is traditionally used to regulate female hormone balance, increase energy and treat gynaecological conditions such as PMS and menopause. It has a long history of use in Asia and is sometimes referred to as the ginseng for women, because of the normalising and stimulating effects felt by women taking the product. It has also been shown clinically to have an effect on stimulating the uterus. Other functions of the botanical include improved peripheral blood circulation, reduction of muscle spasms and relaxation of blood vessels. It is one of the preferred health-promoting herbal supplements for women.

# Echinacea

- Stimulates the immune system
- Purifies the blood
- Stimulates sweat production
- Has antibiotic and antiseptic properties
- Reduces the incidence and duration of common upper respiratory ailments

Echinacea is one of the most common herbs in use today and is even recommended by the World Health Organization. Echinacea extracts have been shown to stimulate immune system function by causing an increase in white blood cells and spleen cells, as well as improved phagocytosis (removal of foreign material from the blood).

**Use:** Clinical studies have shown that taking echinacea extract will reduce the incidence and duration of flu symptoms. It supports immune function during times of physical or emotional stress. As an herbal drug, it is effective as supportive therapy for colds and flu and for chronic infections of the lower urinary tract and respiratory tract, along with appropriate drug therapy.

# Evening Primrose Oil

- **Maintains healthy skin**
- **Soothes PMS-related breast pain**
- **Used to treat eczema**
- **Thins and dilates blood vessels**

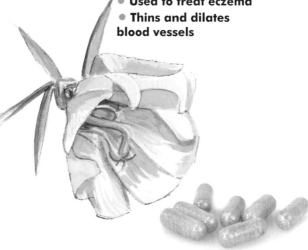

Evening primrose oil is an important source of gamma linolenic acid (GLA), a substance the body needs in order to produce good prostaglandins. Prostaglandins are a group of hormones that regulate many cellular activities. For example, they keep blood platelets from sticking together, control cholesterol formation, reduce inflammation, make insulin work better, improve nerve functioning, regulate calcium metabolism and promote immune system functioning. Evening primrose oil's anti-inflammatory effects may also be helpful for people suffering from rheumatoid arthritis. Ingredients in evening primrose oil have also been shown to thin blood and dilate blood vessels.

# Feverfew

- **Prevents and Relieves chronic migraine pain**
- **Controls inflammation**

The ancient Greeks used feverfew to reduce inflammation and to help control menstrual cramping. Today, the main benefit attributed to this herb is the prevention and relief of migraine, cluster and chronic headaches. The active ingredient in feverfew is parthenolide, a compound that helps control the dilation and constriction of blood vessels in the brain. Used regularly feverfew can prevent migraines from occurring. Most people notice a decrease in migraine attacks after taking feverfew each morning for 2 or more months. Current research suggests that feverfew may have also help relieve inflammatory conditions such as arthritis.

# Fibre

- **Promotes gastrointestinal health**
- **Reduces cholesterol**
- **Aids in weight loss by promoting a feeling of fullness**
- **May prevent degenerative disorders, such as colon cancer**

Insoluble dietary fibre promotes normal elimination by providing bulk for stool formation and thus hastening the passage of the stool through the colon. Insoluble fibre also helps to satisfy appetite by creating a full feeling. Soluble fibre can help to reduce cholesterol levels in the blood. Adequate fibre in the diet will prevent many diet-related health disorders, such as diabetes, coronary heart disease, obesity, high blood pressure and certain cancers.

# Flaxseed Oil

- **Eases constipation**
- **Lowers cholesterol levels**
- **Lowers blood pressure**

Flaxseed oil is found in the seeds of the flax plant.
It is an important source of two essential fatty acids –
linoleic acid and alpha-linolenic acid (ALA). Research
has shown that these ingredients may be helpful in
lowering cholesterol and blood pressure levels.

# Folic Acid

- **Reduces certain birth defects**
  - **Prevents anaemia**
- **Lowers homocysteine levels**
  - **Improves lactation**
  - **Required for cell division**
  - **Useful in controlling pain**
- **Aids in protein metabolism and utilisation of carbohydrates**
- **Essential to formation of red blood cells**

Folic acid is a water-soluble B complex vitamin. It functions in the formation of genetic compounds (DNA and RNA) and participates in metabolic processes. In the body, folic acid is essential for the growth and development of body cells, energy production in the cells and the formation of blood cells. Important for the development of the nervous system in the foetus, taken pre-conceptually and during the first 3 months of pregnancy, folic acid can help prevent certain birth defects such as spina bifida, and decrease the incidence of premature birth. Folic acid is also important for breast feeding mothers.

# Free Radicals

Free radicals are a group of compounds that are
unstable and need to react with other substances in
the body. These uncontrolled oxidations result in
damage to DNA molecules as well as to structures of
the body, such as cell walls, the circulatory system and
nerves. These free radical reactions continue
throughout life and are thought to be responsible for
some of the conditions associated with ageing. Free
radicals can form from normal bodily processes or
when we inhale or absorb environmental pollutants.
Antioxidants neutralise free radicals, and therefore
reduce their damaging effects on the body.

# Garcinia

- **Promotes weight loss**

Garcinia contains a substance called HCA
(hydroxycitric acid or hydroxycitrate). HCA has been
shown to display intriguing anti-obesity functions in
the body. For example, HCA reduces the rate of
formation of fat from carbohydrates by interfering
with an enzyme called ATP-citrate lyase. HCA has also
been found to decrease appetite, and may stimulate
thermogenesis. Garcinia may be useful as a
nutritional weight loss aid and in the maintenance of
desirable body weight.

# Garlic

- **Improves cardiovascular health**
- **Lowers cholesterol levels**
- **Lowers mild elevated blood pressure**
- **Protects blood vessels from free radical damage**
- **Beneficial to the immune system**
- **Helps keep blood fluid**

The phytoactive ingredients in garlic, in particular allicin, display antioxidant activity, slow the development of atherosclerosis, have a mild blood-pressure-lowering effect, reduce blood cholesterol levels, lower triglycerides, inhibit platelet aggregation, lower blood viscosity, stimulate immune system function and exert mild anti-inflammatory effects.

**Use:** Garlic supplements are particularly useful for older people to help maintain fluidity of blood flow, promote heart and circulatory system health and stimulate well-being. Garlic is also recognised for its immune-stimulating properties, and it is traditionally used as an anti-microbial agent.

# Ginger

- **Relieves gastrointestinal discomfort**
- **Promotes circulatory system health**
- **Eases migraine pain**
- **Normalises the nervous system**
- **Reduces LDL cholesterol**
- **Prevents nausea due to motion sickness**

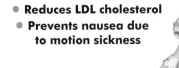

Ginger encourages saliva and gastric juice secretions, reduces stomach and intestinal gas, stimulates intestinal function, and has mild normalising effects on the nervous system. Ginger can be useful to restore gastrointestinal function if you are experiencing discomfort after eating. It is also used to prevent motion sickness.

**Use:** Another potential use for ginger is in the reduction of "bad" LDL cholesterol levels. Finally, ginger may also be useful for sufferers of migraine headaches. Researchers suggest that it may be especially helpful for children who experience migraines because it has a long history of safe use.

# Ginkgo Biloba

- **Improves circulation** - **Sharpens mental acuity** - **Reduces feelings of vertigo** - **Treats headache pain** - **Promotes longevity** - **Relieves muscle pain** - **Inhibits blood clotting** - **Aids with hearing difficulties** - **May treat impotence** - **Increases oxygen supply to the heart**

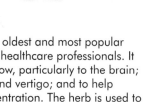

Ginkgo biloba is one of the oldest and most popular herbs, widely prescribed by healthcare professionals. It is taken to improve blood flow, particularly to the brain; to ease anxiety, confusion and vertigo; and to help improve memory and concentration. The herb is used to treat memory disorders, lack of concentration, dizziness, tinnitus and headaches. Ginkgo is available as a standardised extract of 24% ginkgoflavoneglycosides.

**Use:** Ginkgo biloba appears to make the blood less sticky and so improves circulation. It is also an antioxidant and can be beneficial in maintaining health and promoting longevity. Although popularly used to improve brain function and memory, studies of patients undergoing walking rehabilitation showed that the subjects taking ginkgo experienced significant improvements including increased walking distance and reduced leg pain. This may indicate possible benefits of ginkgo supplement use for exercisers and athletes. Persons using anti-coagulants or bloodthinning drugs should consult their doctor before taking this supplement.

# Ginseng

- **Fights fatigue**
- **Creates feeling of well-being**
- **Decreases blood pressure**
- **Boosts immune system**
- **Increases cognitive function**
- **Assists with gastrointestinal problems**
- **Aids with arthritis pain**
- **May help diabetics maintain blood glucose levels**

There are three main ginseng plants that you will find used in nutritional supplements: Asian (or Korean) ginseng (Panax ginseng) and American ginseng (Panax quinquefolius), which are the true ginsengs and Siberian ginseng (Eleutherococcus senticosus). Asian ginseng is said to be the strongest of the three; the root of the plant has been used for more than 2,000 years to help treat a variety of conditions. American ginseng is milder than its Asian cousin and, as a result, it is the preferred treatment for elderly patients.

Siberian ginseng has a more modern usage – the Russians popularised it during the 20th century to improve the performance of their athletes and workforce. Its use developed primarily as an alternative to Panax ginseng. Siberian ginseng is used to relieve stress, enhance mental function and improve physical endurance.

**Use:** As a group, the ginsengs produce a diverse number of benefits, based on the so-called adaptogenic effects for which the ginsengs are noted. These benefits include: improving physical and mental energy, reducing feelings of fatigue and burnout, increasing work capacity, improving concentration, stimulating the immune system, increasing alertness, improving reaction time and increasing co-ordination.

# Glucosamine Sulphate
## (Sulfate, HCl)

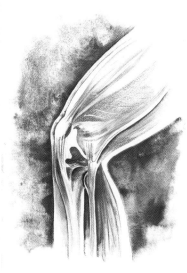

- **Treats the painful symptoms of osteoarthritis**
- **Promotes wound healing**
- **Strengthens circulatory system health**
- **Improves the appearance of skin, hair and nails**
- **Stimulates production of connective tissues**
- **Improves joint repair and function**

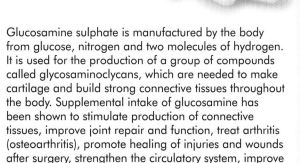

Glucosamine sulphate is manufactured by the body from glucose, nitrogen and two molecules of hydrogen. It is used for the production of a group of compounds called glycosaminoclycans, which are needed to make cartilage and build strong connective tissues throughout the body. Supplemental intake of glucosamine has been shown to stimulate production of connective tissues, improve joint repair and function, treat arthritis (osteoarthritis), promote healing of injuries and wounds after surgery, strengthen the circulatory system, improve joint lubrication, and improve the thickness of skin, nails and hair.

# Gotu Kola

- **Maintains vascular health**
- **Improves circulation**
- **Supports the growth and repair of tissues and skin**
- **Improves mental function**
- **Improves skin appearance**
- **May help fight cellulite**

Gotu kola contains a group of phytonutrients called asiaticosides, which are thought to stimulate tissue growth, in particular in the skin, connective tissues, and capillaries. Gotu kola is used in nutritional supplements to maintain vascular health, and support the growth and repair of connective tissues and skin. Recent studies have reported on gotu kola's possible role in improving mental function in children and adults. Gotu kola improves skin appearance and may be used as nutritional support in the treatment of skin diseases and venous insufficiency.

# Grape Seed Extract

- **Supports circulatory system health**
- **May prevent certain degenerative diseases**
- **Maintains young-looking skin**
- **Promotes lung health**
- **Has anti-inflammatory, anti- histamine and anti-ulcer properties**
- **Fights cavities and gum disease**
- **A potent antioxidant**

The phyto nutrients contained in grape seed extract have powerful antioxidant action; these nutrients inhibit enzymes that breakdown and damage blood vessels, connective tissues and skin, whilst maintaining the flexibility of blood vessels. Grape seed extract should be included as a daily supplement. Many comprehensive antioxidant formulas will contain grape seed extract with other botanical antioxidants. Grape skin extract is also available: it has similar benefits to grape seed extract.

**Use:** Grape seed extract is an antioxidant which promotes health and well-being. It stimulates, supports and maintains circulatory system health. It also can be used as nutritional support for venous or circulatory system diseases.

# Guarana

- **Improves concentration**
- **Reduces appetite**
- **Delays sleep**
- **Increases endurance**
- **May prevent the effects of a hangover**

Guarana has a long history of safe use in South America. It is sold in beverages similar to colas, and is used to stimulate mental and physical energy. It contains caffeine and other related methylxanthines, such as theobromine and theophylline, which are central nervous system stimulants and have a mild diuretic effect. The methylxanthines also stimulate an increase in your fat-burning rate and may reduce appetite in some people.

# Horse Chestnut

- **Promotes vein structure and function**
- **Helps in the management of varicose veins**
- **Reduces leg pain**
- **Treats oedema**
- **May help treat cellulite**

Horse chestnut seed supplements are known
for their vascular system tightening effects. These
improvements in vascular system structure are thought
to be due to horse chestnut seed's stabilising effect
on cell membranes and normalising effect on
capillary tone. It is best known for its use in preventing
and treating varicose veins and haemorrhoids.

# Iron

- **Prevents anaemia**
- **Improves immune system health**
- **Aids growth**
- **Necessary for proper skin tone**
- **Prevents fatigue**

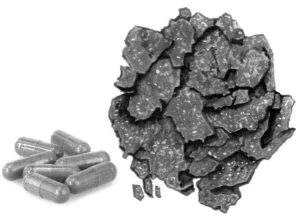

Iron is best known for its essential oxygen transport role as part of haemoglobin in the blood, and myoglobin in the muscles. Iron is found in a number of enzymes and is stored in bone marrow, and liver and spleen tissues. Pregnant and menstruating women, athletes, vegetarians, senior citizens, and infants who are being fed cow's milk are especially at risk from low iron levels, one of the world's most common nutritional deficiencies. Iron supplements are very important to these groups because very little of the iron we need can be obtained from the foods we eat. One of the richest dietary sources of iron is red meat, and the body can only absorb about 10% to 20% of the meat's iron content. Taken daily this supplement prevents iron deficiency anaemia and impaired immune function.

# Kava Kava

- **Has a calming effect**
- **Prevents insomnia**
- **Effective for treating and relieving anxiety in adults**
- **Reduces anxiety and depression in menopausal women**

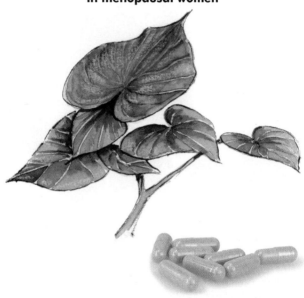

Kava kava root extract has been shown to have calming, anti-anxiety, mild sedative, muscle relaxing, and local anesthetic effects. It also stimulates better concentration. It can be beneficial for menopausal women and in a study of forty patients, kava kava extract reduced the severity of symptoms associated with menopause, including depression and anxiety.

# Kelp

- **Excellent source of iodine**
- **Used in weight loss**
- **Detoxifies**

Kelp is rich in iodine, an essential part of the thyroid hormones thyroxine and triiodothyronine, and vital for proper thyroid gland functioning. The thyroid gland regulates normal metabolism, growth and energy production. Most vitamin-mineral supplements contain iodine, with a safe history of use. Some weight loss supplements and aids also contain Kelp to stimuate the metabolism. Kelp is also used in detoxification supplements as it has the unique property of binding with heavy metals and organic substances such as cholesterol. Also contains B complex vitamins and minerals including calcium, potassium, phosphorus and magnesium. Kelp is a seaweed extract.

# Lecithin

- **Supports brain health**
- **Maintains liver and heart health**
- **Improves physical performance**
- **Reduces cholesterol levels**

Lecithin is a type of phospholipid that has a molecule of choline attached to the phosphate molecule. Lecithin supplies the body with the essential nutrient choline and is involved in important biological functions, including: brain development, learning and fertility. It can help lower serum cholesterol, improve short-term memory, improve endurance, serve as a precursor to the important neurotransmitter acetylcholine and prevent fatty liver.

**Use:** Lecithin supplements have been much used in the last fifty years. Clinical studies have verified that blood levels of choline are maintained at a higher level for a longer time when derived from lecithin than from choline chloride.

# Lutein

- **Improves vision**
- **Supports circulatory system health**
- **Improves immune system function**

Lutein is a carotenoid that functions as an antioxidant. It has been shown to have special benefits in improving vision, maintaining circulatory system health and supporting immune system function.

# Lycopene

**• May reduce the risk of certain cancers**

Lycopene is a phyto nutrient and a carotenoid found in tomatoes. Lycopene functions as an antioxidant and is reportedly more potent than Vitamin E and other carotenoids, such as beta-carotene. Lycopene became popular in recent years following a Havard University study which found a significant association between the consumption of tomatoes and reduced cancer risk; in particular prostate cancer. The nutrient has been shown to be beneficial in treating or reducing the risk of a number of cancers, most notably prostate and lung cancers, but including cancers of the colon, pancreas and cervix. Lycopene may also be beneficial in promoting cardiovascular wellness and preventing other degenerative diseases.

# Magnesium

- **Vital to good health and energy production**
- **May ward off depression**
- **Promotes heart and circulatory system health**
- **Improves physical performance and weight loss**
- **Alleviates PMS symptoms**
- **Reduces muscle spasms**

Magnesium is an important structural component of bone and is involved in many metabolic reactions, including energy production and synthesis of proteins and nucleic acids. It plays a role in the relaxation of muscle tissues and the maintenance of heart health and function. Improvements in athletic performance have recently been reported among athletes taking magnesium supplements. Women who experience menstrual discomfort can also benefit from supplemental intake of magnesium.

# Manganese

**● Maintains bones and connective tissue**

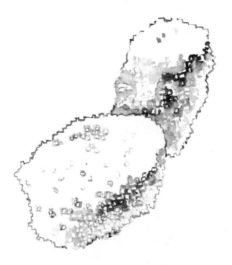

Manganese is an essential trace mineral required
for energy production. It is a component of enzymes
and the antioxidant superoxide dismutase (SOD).
Manganese aids in bone and connective tissue
formation. It is one of the key trace minerals essential
for health and well-being.

# Mastika

- **Eases gastric ulcers**
- **Has antioxidant properties**
- **May decrease blood pressure**
- **Has anti-bacterial properties**

Mastic resin has been used for centuries in a diverse number of applications. The ancient Egyptians used the resin as an incense and embalming agent. Other cultures have used the oil and resin as a breath freshener, chewing gum ingredient and flavouring for alcoholic beverages. Mastika is made up of more than 70 ingredients, which may account for its varied uses.

Mastika may be used to aid in the treatment of gastric ulcers as studies show that it can destroy Heliobacter pylori, the bacterium associated with stomach ulcers. Scientists have also suggested that mastika may have anti-bacterial, antioxidant and anti-hypertensive effects.

# Molybdenum

### • Essential for good health

Molybdenum is an essential trace mineral found in small amounts in the body. It is present in enzymes that are involved in energy production, uric acid formation and nitrogen metabolism. Molybdenum intake has been determined to be essential for good health.

# MSM

- **Promotes joint health**
- **Promotes healthy immune system function**
- **Maintains healthy gastrointestinal and respiratory tracts**
- **Essential for healthy skin, hair and joints**

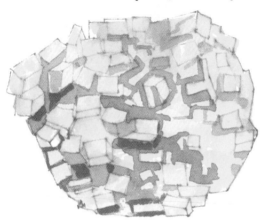

MSM (or methylsulfonylmethane) is a sulphur-containing substance that occurs naturally in plants and animals. MSM serves as a supply of biologically accessible sulphur, to be used in structural proteins and enzymes. MSM's most noted use as a nutritional supplement is with connective tissue disorders and arthritis as studies have shown that MSM stimulates collagen formation. MSM also plays a role in promoting immune system function by supplying the sulphur needed in the formation of IgG, an important immunoglobulin. MSM supplements support the proper structure and function of the gastrointestinal and respiratory tracts   MSM promotes the growth and maintenance of connective tissues, resulting in improvements in joints, skin, hair, and other tissues.

# Muira Puama

- **Eases PMS symptoms**
- **Treats erectile dysfunction**

Muira puama, also known as "potency wood," has a long history of use as an aphrodisiac. The roots and bark of this flowering shrub, indigenous to the Brazilian Amazon, are traditionally brewed into a tea to treat erectile dysfunction as well as a number of other ailments. Europeans arriving on the South American continent learned of this ancient remedy from the native Brazilian people. The explorers brought this knowledge home with them and, today, muira puama is listed in the British Herbal Pharmacopeia as an approved treatment for erectile dysfunction.

# Nickel

- **Needed for good health**

Nickel is present in all the tissues of the body. It is found firmly attached to DNA, and there is even a protein that binds to it in the blood. Deficiency in animals impairs iron absorption.

# Noni

- **Traditionally used for a number of ailments including constipation, wounds and fevers.**
- **May support heart, liver and kidney health**

Noni is a small shrub that is native to Asia, Australia and the Pacific Islands. Traditionally, noni (also known as morinda or Indian mulberry) has been used to treat a number of health disorders. Polynesians take the herb to alleviate digestive disorders, skin inflammation and wounds. In Traditional Chinese Medicine, noni is used to strengthen the immune and digestive systems and support the heart, liver and kidneys.Studies indicate that noni can help inflammatory conditions such as arthritis, headaches, and allergies.

# Omega-3 Fatty Acids

- **Maintains joint flexibility**
- **Promotes longevity**
- **Builds healthy bones, skin, hair and nails**
- **Promotes a healthy heart and circulatory system**

Omega-3 fatty acids such as EPA and DHA are found in fish oils. These two substances are linked with lowering triglycerides – thus helping to prevent heart disease – and inhibiting atherosclerosis (hardening of the arteries), and helping to reduce pain and inflammation. Omega-3 fatty acids are the ideal supplement for anyone seeking to maintain optimum health.

# Phosphorus

- **Important part of bone structure**
- **Essential for energy production**

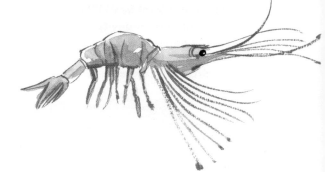

Phosphorus is an important part of bone and is also found in lipids, cell membranes, nucleic acids and proteins. It is present in all cells and occurs as phosphate or combined with other elements in body fluids, such as sodium phosphate or dyhydrogen phosphate. It is part of the body's primary energy molecule, ATP (adenosine tri phosphate). Phosphorus is required for health, and maintenance of structure and function of the body.

# Potassium

- **Improves physical performance**
  - **Maintains overall health**

Potassium is an essential mineral and a major component of all cells. It helps maintain fluid balance in the body, and functions in nerve transmissions, regulation of heartbeat, muscle contractions, and glycogen formation. Adequate potassium intake maintains health and improves physical performance.

# Probiotics/ Prebiotics

- **Supports digestive system health**

Probiotics are supplements containing the beneficial microflora (bacteria) that normally inhabit a healthy digestive system. Generally used to promote digestive system health and normal function, they may also correct both constipation and diarrhoea.

# Red Clover

- **Eases menopausal symptoms**
- **Has anti-ageing effects**
- **Supports cardiovascular health**
- **Builds strong bones**
- **May reduce the risk of developing certain cancers**

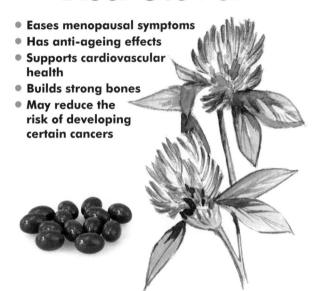

Red clover is beneficial because of the plant's high concentration of isoflavones. Isoflavones are a unique group of plant nutrients found in high amounts in certain plants, such as red clover, soy and kudzu root. These plants contain a number of isoflavones, but the two most important and most potent are genistein and daidzein. During the past two decades, researchers have linked the consumption of diets rich in isoflavones with health-promoting effects, including relieving uncomfortable symptoms associated with menopause; anti-ageing effects; improving cardiovascular health; bone building; and reduction of certain cancers.
Along with characteristic antioxidant properties, the isoflavones also exhibit oestrogen-like activity. This phytoestrogenic effect is particularly important because it has been shown to ease the symptoms of menopause for millions of women.

# Red Yeast Rice

- **Lowers cholesterol levels**
- **Promotes cardiovascular health**

Originating in China, red yeast rice (also called Monascus purpureus) is a type of yeast that, when fermented on rice, results in the production of natural statin-type chemicals, similar to the drug Lovastatin. Several clinical studies conducted in China indicate that taking as little as 1,200 mg of standardised red rice yeast supplement significantly lowered blood cholesterol levels within eight weeks, with no side effects. A recent clinical study conducted in the United States using 2,400 mg of standardised red rice yeast confirmed these results.

# Royal Jelly

- **Improves energy levels** • **Increases mental acuity** • **May improve sexual function**
- **Maintains healthy, young-looking skin**
- **Fights mild depression and anxiety** • **Helps promote liver health** • **Aids in weight control**
- **Provides support during menopause** • **Eases joint pain** • **Lowers cholesterol levels** • **Has anti-bacterial properties**

Fresh royal jelly is a milky, white substance created by the glands of worker bees. This nutrient-rich liquid is fed to bee larvae for the first few days of their lives to ensure their good health and survival. However, only the queen bee will partake of the hormonally rich jelly throughout her life. Queen bees grow larger and live longer than other bees, which led health practitioners to believe that chemicals in royal jelly increased longevity. Royal jelly also makes queen bees extremely fertile – allowing them to produce up to two-and-a-half times their body weight in eggs daily. The active ingredients of royal jelly have never been fully

**Use:** Royal jelly has been used to treat rheumatoid arthritis, high cholesterol levels, kidney and liver disorders, insomnia and fatigue, loss of appetite in infants and the elderly, stomach ulcers and, more recently, jet-lag. Royal jelly is also used in skin care products and to combat the effects of ageing. You will most often find royal jelly in energy products and health tonics. Connoisseurs of health prefer fresh royal jelly.

# SAMe

- **Eases arthritis pain and inflammation**
- **Alleviates feelings of depression and anxiety**

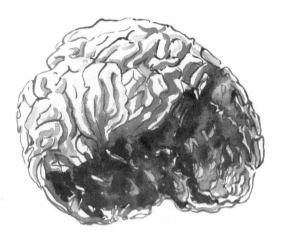

SAMe (s-adenosylmethionine) is a compound that occurs naturally in our bodies, but as we age we produce less and less  not enough is produced for adequate health. SAMe is essential to healthy activity in all human cells and plays a central role in hundreds of metabolic reactions. It is even involved in the production of glucosamine, which researchers believe helps make SAMe beneficial to joint function. SAMe also aids the body by producing brain chemicals which help promote an energetic outlook on life and relieve depression. SAMe can be taken along with glucosamine sulphate, MSM and chondroitin sulphate.

# Saw Palmetto

- **Promotes prostate health**
- **Reduces prostate inflammation**

In over twenty-two clinical studies, saw palmetto extract has been shown to promote the health and function of the prostate in adult males. Saw palmetto extract has been reported in clinical studies to be an effective treatment for non malignant prostate conditions, such as benign prostatic hyperplasia (BPH). In studies of BPH, saw palmetto extract was shown to improve urine flow, decrease prostate size, reduce inflammation, reduce frequency of urination at night, improve duration of bladder voiding, and reduce post-micturitional dribbling. Results are seen in four to six weeks, with progressive improvements seen with continued use.

# Selenium

- **Powerful antioxidant**
- **Helps guard against certain cancers**
- **Promotes heart health**
- **Alleviates hot flushes**
- **Promotes longevity**
- **Maintains prostate health**

Selenium is a component of one of the body's major antioxidants, glutathione peroxidase. Glutathione peroxidase protects the body from free-radical damage. In its role as an antioxidant co-factor, selenium reduces the risk of degenerative diseases such as heart disease, arthritis, and certain cancers. In fact, the association between adequate selenium intake and a reduced cancer risk has recently garnered media coverage. Selenium's role as an antioxidant co-factor is extremely important, and new research has confirmed its role in strengthening the body to reduce the risk of cancer.

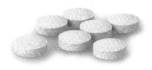

# Soy

- **Promotes cardiovascular wellness**
  - **Supports digestive health**
- **Eases menopausal symptoms**

Consumption of soybeans, and soybean-derived products has been associated with many health benefits, including reduction of the risk of cancer and cardiovascular diseases. The research concerning these beneficial health effects is impressive. Soy is loaded with healthy essential nutrients, including protein, essential fatty acids, fibre, vitamins and minerals. It also contains an interesting group of health-promoting and protective bioflavonoids, called isoflavones. The specific type of isoflavones found in soy exhibit antioxidant activity and phytoestrogenic activity. This phytoestrogenic effect is responsible for soy's reduction of the severity of symptoms during menopause. Soy also has been shown to help normalise gastrointestinal function. Finally, ingestion of soy products is associated with lower cancer risk, probably because of the phyto nutrients content.

# St John's Wort

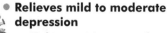

- **Relieves mild to moderate depression**
- **Helps repair nerve damage**
- **Calms nervous conditions**
- **Relieves insomnia**
- **Exhibits anti-viral and anti-fungal properties**
- **Reduces menstrual cramping**

Many clinical studies have confirmed that the herb St John's wort (hypericum perforatum) can have anti-depressant action. It has been discovered to be an effective treatment for mild to moderate depression. The herb also reduces anxiety and unrest in some people and has been used to alleviate SAD (Seasonal Affective Disorder). The supplement is usually available as a standardised extract of hypericin, the active ingredient.

**Use:** Studies reveal that the standardised extracts of hypericin will normalise serotonin levels and GABA activity (a calming nervous system substance), and help normalise the norepinephrine and dopamine systems. Its immuno-modulating effects may also contribute to its anti-depressant action, making it the most broad-spectrum anti-depressant medication known. Widely prescribed in Germany and northern Europe, St John's Wort is one of the major herbal supplements. St John's wort may affect the way in which some prescribed medicines work and may cause photosensitivity in fair-skinned people.

# Starflower Oil

- **Rich source of GLA**
- **Promotes healthy skin**
- **Relieves rheumatoid arthritis pain**
- **Promotes hormonal balance**

Starflower oil, also known as borage, is an important source of gamma linolenic acid (GLA), a substance the body needs in order to produce prostaglandins. Prostaglandins are a group of hormones that regulate many cellular activities. For example, they keep blood platelets from sticking together, control cholesterol formation, reduce inflammation, make insulin work better, improve nerve functioning, regulate calcium metabolism and promote immune system functioning. Starflower oil has been used in clinical trials to ease the symptoms of eczema and other skin ailments and rheumatoid arthritis.

# Tin

**Useful for good health**

Tin is a trace element that is often found in nutritional supplement products. Trace elements are substances that have been found occurring in the human body in extremely small amounts.

# Valerian

- **Effective sleep aid for adults**
- **Eases PMS-related pain**
- **Soothes gall bladder and kidney stone pain**
- **Has analgesic and anti-spasmodic effects**

Valerian has sedative and sleep-promoting actions.
It is reported to promote good-quality sleep, without
the hangover side effect sometimes experienced with
prescription and over-the-counter sleep aid drugs.
Note that valerian is strong smelling; some companies
add vanilla or peppermint to mask this smell.
However, the odour is an indication that you are
getting a high-quality product.

# Vanadium

- **Essential for healthy bones and teeth**
- **Needed for growth and reproduction**
- **May increase glucose utilisation**

Vanadium is a trace mineral present in the body in
minute amounts. Vanadium is involved in metabolic
pathways and is needed for cellular metabolism,
for the formation of bones and teeth and for growth
and reproduction. Recent attention has been focused
on vanadium's role in glucose metabolism and its
insulin-mimetic effects, which may increase glucose
utilisation. Vanadium is also known to inhibit
cholesterol synthesis at pharmacological dosages.
Adequate dietary vanadium intake is required for
maintenance of good health.

# Vitamin A

- **Supports eye health**
- **Improves immune and respiratory system function**
- **Promotes healthy skin**
- **Has antioxidant capabilities**
- **Promotes growth**
- **May help treat emphysema and hyperthyroidism**

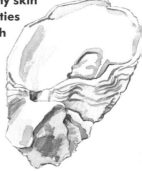

Vitamin A is an essential fat-soluble vitamin required for maintenance of normal mucous membranes and for normal vision. Vitamin A refers to a group of compounds that display vitamin A activity. Retinol is the principal vitamin A and belongs to a class of chemicals known as the retinoids. Retinol and other retinoids occur in animal tissues. Beta-carotene, and other carotenoids, also display vitamin A activity, and are sometimes referred to as provitamin A, because they are converted to vitamin A in the body as needed. Carotenoids occur in plants and have the added benefit of providing antioxidant activity.

**Use:** Supplementary intake of vitamin A is known to improve immune function, improve day and night vision, reduce eye fatigue, and improve skin function and structure. Vitamin A therapy is used in the treatment of skin disorders such as acne, eczema and psoriasis. It is also used as supportive therapy in the treatment of respiratory illnesses such as allergies, asthma, bronchitis and emphysema.

# Vitamin B1
## *(Thiamine)*

- **Promotes nervous system health**
  - **Aids in digestion**
  - **Promotes growth**
  - **Soothes stress**
- **Keeps the heart and muscles working properly**

Vitamin B1 is a water-soluble vitamin involved in many metabolic reactions. It is converted in the body into co-enzymes that aid in carbohydrate metabolism. Vitamin B1 also functions in the production of ribose, which is needed for the production of RNA and DNA. It is also involved in maintenance of nervous system functioning.

# Vitamin B2
## *(Riboflavin)*

- **Eases stress**
- **Promotes good vision**
- **Strengthens hair and nails and promotes healthy skin**
- **Soothes sore mouth, lips and tongue**
- **Helps metabolise the major food groups**

Vitamin B2 is an essential water-soluble vitamin.
It is involved in the production of energy from
carbohydrates, fatty acids, and amino acids. Vitamin
B2 is involved in the regeneration of one of the body's
important antioxidants, glutathione. Adequate intake
of the vitamin is essential for good health.

# Vitamin B3
## *(Niacin)*

- **Aids in digestion**
- **Reduces cholesterol levels**
- **Increases energy and circulation**
- **Helps to reduce blood pressure**
- **Promotes healthy skin**
- **Required for the synthesis of sex hormones, cortisone, insulin and thyroxin**

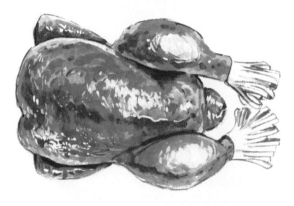

Vitamin B3 is a water-soluble essential vitamin. It is functionally active as part of two important co-enzymes – nicotinamide adenine dinucleotide (NAD) and nicotinamine adenine dinucleotide phosphate (NADP). These two enzymes are present in every living cell and involved in many vital metabolic processes including energy production, fatty acid production, glycolysis, and the reduction of cholesterol and fatty acids in the blood stream. Vitamin B3 supplementation was shown to reduce "bad" LDL-cholesterol, while increasing "good" HDL-cholesterol.

# Vitamin B5
## (Pantothenic acid)

- **Essential for energy production**
- **Supports adrenal glands**
- **Strengthens the immune system**
- **Maintains normal growth and development**

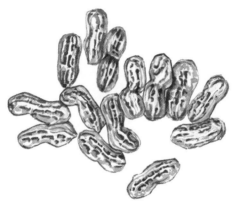

Vitamin B5 is essential for good health, production of energy, and production of hormones; it is an essential water-soluble vitamin. It has many important metabolic functions, primarily as a component of co-enzyme A. Co-enzyme A is important the Krebs cycle (one of the body's energy producing pathways) and in the metabolism of fatty acids. This makes vitamin B5 important in the production of energy from carbohydrates and fatty acids. It is also involved in cholesterol and steroid synthesis.

# Vitamin B6
## *(Pyridoxine)*

- **Metabolises fats and protein**
- **Eases muscle pain**
- **Maintains healthy skin**
- **Produces antibodies**
- **Assimilates protein and fats**
- **Essential for the proper absorption**

Vitamin B6 is an essential water-soluble vitamin. It maintains good health, boosts immunity, protects against development of some nervous system disorders, and is used in the nutritional treatment of PMS and carpal tunnel syndrome.

# Vitamin B12
## *(Cyanocobalamin)*

- **Improves cognitive abilities**
- **Relieves mild depression**
- **Maintains thyroid function**
- **Promotes cardiovascular health**
- **Aids in the production of red blood cells**
- **Stimulates energy**

Vitamin B12 is an essential water-soluble vitamin, required for healthy metabolism and proper nerve function. Vitamin B12 functions is important for new cell growth, nerve tissue development, folate metabolism (which is important to maintain healthy homocysteine levels), DNA synthesis, and energy production. It is also required for the production of red blood cells. In addition to Vitamin B12's role in maintaining overall health, its use as an energy enhancer is of interest to athletes, the elderly, and anyone who is experiencing low energy levels. Also, the vitamin's role in maintaining homocysteine levels is vital to cardiovascular health.

# Vitamin C
## *(Ascorbic acid)*

- Accelerates wound healing
- Eases stress • Lowers cholesterol
- Strengthens the immune system
- Produces collagen
- Acts as an anti-histamine
- Helps the body absorb iron
- Promotes longevity
- Essential for overall health
- Can decrease cancer risk

Vitamin C is a water-soluble essential vitamin that functions primarily in the production of collagen, the intercellular tissues that hold the body's cells together. It also helps heal wounds, fights infection, maintains healthy capillaries, and promotes healthy gums and teeth. Vitamin C is a very important antioxidant and protects cells from damage; it also prevents the oxidation of folate. It assists in the metabolism of tyrosine and phenylalanine, and aids in the absorption of iron.

**Use:** An adequate vitamin C intake is necessary for good health and protection from free radical damage. Vitamin C is commonly used as supportive nutritional therapy in the treatment of several disorders, including bleeding gums, the common cold, allergies, asthma, and emotional stress. It is also thought to promote cardiovascular wellness and protect against cancer.

# Vitamin D

- **Builds strong bones and teeth**
- **Osteoporosis prevention**
- **Cancer prevention**
- **Builds a healthy immune system**
- **Aids in the assimilation of vitamin A**
- **Relieves the symptoms of psoriasis**
- **Promotes healthy joints**
- **May help fight the common cold**

Vitamin D is known as the "sunshine vitamin" because it is produced when the body is exposed to the sun's ultraviolet B (UVB) rays. It is a fat-soluble vitamin, meaning that it is dissolved in the body's fatty tissues. The liver and kidney help convert vitamin D to its active hormone form. As people age their need for vitamin D supplementation increases. Studies show that taking vitamin D supplements provides health benefits to people of all ages – in particular building and maintaining strong bones.

**Use:** Produced naturally in the body, vitamin D may offer protection against certain types of cancer, specifically breast, colon and prostate cancer; reduction in joint damage due to arthritis; relief from the symptoms of psoriasis (a skin disorder); can improve immune system function; and protection against the nerve disorder multiple sclerosis.

# Vitamin E

- **Powerful antioxidant**
- **Heals scar tissue**
- **Helps lower blood pressure**
- **Protects lungs against pollution**
- **Promotes cardiovascular wellness**
- **Mild anti-inflammatory effects**
- **Maintains immune system function**
- **Retards cellular ageing**

Vitamin E is an essential fat-soluble nutrient. It is mainly known for its role as an antioxidant, protecting the body from free radical damage. This antioxidant function contributes to a reduced risk of developing certain degenerative diseases, such as coronary heart disease, cataracts, certain cancers, and arthritis; it also protects tissue lipids and vitamin A from oxidation.

**Use:** Vitamin E enhances the action of the immune system. It lessens the severity of inflammation and premenstrual syndrome and helps improve circulatory irregularities such as nocturnal leg cramps and blood platelet adhesion. Vitamin E inhibits the conversion of dietary nitrites to harmful nitrosamines in the stomach. Nitrosamines are strong tumor promoters and implicated in causing gastrointestinal cancers.

# Vitamin K

- **Essential for circulatory health**
- **May prevent osteoporosis**
- **Vital for healing bone fractures**

Vitamin K is an essential lipid-soluble vitamin that functions in the synthesis of prothrombin, a substance that is vital for blood clotting. Without vitamin K, the blood clotting process cannot be initiated. Individuals, who are physically active, involved in athletics or who are employed in physical jobs where bumps and bruises frequently occur could benefit from supplemental intake of vitamin K.

# Wild Yam

- **Promotes hormonal balance**
- **Eases PMS symptoms**
- **Soothes uterine and gastrointestinal distress**
- **Useful in the treatment of rheumatoid arthritis**
- **Eases nervous excitement**

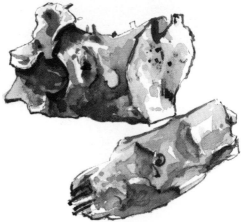

Mexican wild yam is a phytonutrient whose active ingredient, diosgenin, is a natural progesterone. Traditionally used as a remedy for infertility, impotence and uterine pain, Mexican Yam was used in the manufacture of the original birth control pill. It has the ability to regulate hormone levels and is particularly beneficial to women who suffer from PMS, menopausal symptoms and other gynaecological discomfort. Also an anti-inflammatory, especially for gastrointestinal pain and rheumatoid arthritis. Do not confuse with the popular vegetable, Yam or Sweet Potato.

# Zinc

- Promotes prostate health
- Improves vision
- Enhances wound healing
- Supports a healthy immune system
- Essential for protein synthesis
- Necessary for fertility
- Vital for the taste mechanism
- Needed for proper brain function

Zinc is a component of over two hundred enzymes that play important roles in cell replication, tissue repair, and growth. Zinc is also involved in the production, storage, and secretion of hormones, including testosterone and growth hormone. It is well known for its role in reproductive system health and prostate gland functioning.

**Use:** Maintaining adequate zinc status is vital for good health. Improved immune function, healing, fertility, skin health and vision are just some of the benefits. Zinc supplementation also can restore or improve the sense of taste and smell in some individuals with zinc deficiency.

# Section Two:

## Nutritional Supplement Use

This section includes information on which supplement ingredients medical research has shown to be effective in maintaining and promoting health.

- Daily Supplement Plan
- Memory
- Anti-Ageing
- Menopause
- Colds/Flu
- Men's Health
- Circulation
- PMS

- Depression
- Skin Care
- Digestion
- Sleep Problems
- Energy
- Slimming
- Healthy Heart
- Stress/Anxiety

# Daily Supplement Plan

The following supplements should be taken on a daily basis for overall well-being and good health.

- Beta-carotene
- Biotin
- Boron
- Calcium
- Chloride
- Chromium
- Co-Enzyme Q10
- Copper
- Fibre
- Folic Acid
- Ginkgo Biloba
- Grape Seed Extract
- Iron
- Lutein
- Lycopene
- Magnesium
- Manganese
- Molybdenum
- Omega-3 Fatty Acids
- Phosphorus
- Potassium
- Probiotics/Prebiotics
- Selenium
- Vitamin A
- Vitamin B1
- Vitamin B2
- Vitamin B3
- Vitamin B5
- Vitamin B6
- Vitamin B12
- Vitamin C
- Vitamin D
- Vitamin E
- Vitamin K
- Zinc

# Anti-Ageing

As we get older, our health and nutrition needs change. Our bodies do not digest many of the essential nutrients we need to remain healthy as readily as they used to. As a result, supplementation with certain vitamins, minerals and botanicals becomes essential to looking and feeling your best. Maintaining an adequate intake of antioxidant nutrients becomes especially important during this stage of your life. Antioxidants such as vitamins C and E, and beta-carotene are important for their anti-ageing effects on the body.

Some of the concerns faced by older people include: vision health; hearing difficulties and loss; circulatory system health; improving mental acuity and concentration; preventing osteoporosis; and maintaining healthy, young-looking skin.

| SUPPLEMENT | COMMENTS |
|---|---|
| Arginine | Promotes longevity |
| Beta-carotene | A powerful antioxidant; may prevent certain types of cancer; decreases risk of certain eye disorders |
| Calcium | Builds strong bones and prevents osteoporosis |
| Cat's Claw | Promotes longevity |
| CO-Q10 | Antioxidant and energy factor |
| Cranberry | Maintains bladder and kidney health |
| Fibre | May prevent certain degenerative diseases |
| Garlic | Keeps circulatory system healthy |

| | |
|---|---|
| Ginkgo Biloba | Aids with memory, hearing and circulation difficulties |
| Ginseng | Increases energy and cognitive function |
| Glucosamine | Improves connective tissue health, and appearance of skin, hair and nails |
| Grape seed Extract | Maintains young-looking skin |
| Iron | Oxygenates blood |
| Lutein | Improves vision |
| Molybdenum5.5 | Essential for good health |
| MSM | Essential for healthy skin |
| Omega-3 Fatty Acids | Promotes longevity |
| Red Clover | Source of natural oestrogen |
| Royal Jelly | For energy and young-looking skin |
| Selenium | A powerful antioxidant |
| Vitamin A | Supports vision health |
| Vitamin B2 | Promotes good vision |
| Vitamin B6 | Maintains healthy skin |
| Vitamin B12 | Improves energy and cognitive abilities |
| Vitamin C | Essential for good health; promotes longevity |
| Vitamin D | Builds strong bones |
| Vitamin E | A powerful antioxidant; retards cellular ageing |
| Vitamin K | May prevent osteoporosis |
| Zinc | Improves immunity |

# Arthritis

One of the most encouraging developments of the 1990s was the discovery that osteoporosis – a decrease in bone mass and density – can be prevented. In fact, bone strength and density can be restored through nutritional means. Similarly, connective tissues, such as cartilage and ligaments, respond favorably to nutritional supplements. As we age, our body's capacity to maintain and build connective tissues diminishes. If dietary measures are not taken to provide essential building blocks for these important tissues, degenerative diseases such as arthritis may develop. Clinical studies conducted throughout the world have shown that the body will respond positively to nutritional therapy and actually repair degenerated tissues over a course of several weeks to several months.

People suffering from conditions such as osteoarthritis often have to combat the inflammation that may accompany these problems. There are a number of dietary supplements that can help reduce inflammation and serve as an alternative to pharmaceutical drugs.

| SUPPLEMENT | COMMENTS |
| --- | --- |
| Boron | Supports bone health |
| Calcium | Prevents osteoporosis |
| Chondroitin Sulphate | Eases osteoarthritis pain |
| CMO | Helps to normalize immune system function |
| Copper | Keeps bones healthy |
| Devil's Claw | Eases pain<br>Controls inflammation |

| | |
|---|---|
| **Feverfew** | Controls inflammation |
| **Ginger** | Has anti-inflammatory properties |
| **Ginseng** | Aids with arthritis pain |
| **Glucosamine Sulphate** | Improves joint repair and function |
| **Gotu Kola** | Supports the growth and repair of tissues |
| **Manganese** | Maintains bones and connective tissue |
| **MSM** | Promotes joint health |
| **Omega-3 Fatty Acids** | Controls pain and inflammation |
| **Phosphorus** | Important part of bone structure |
| **Red Clover** | Builds bone |
| **Royal Jelly** | Eases joint pain |
| **SAMe** | Eases arthritis pain and inflammation |
| **St John's Wort** | Reduces inflammation |
| **Starflower Oil** | Relieves rheumatoid arthritis pain |
| **Vanadium** | Essential for healthy bones |
| **Vitamin D** | Used for osteoporosis prevention |
| **Vitamin K** | May prevent osteoporosis |
| **Wild Yam** | Reduces inflammation |

# Colds/Flu

While eating the right food and taking nutritional supplements are important for a properly functioning immune system (and remember that a poor diet, with too much fat, alcohol, sugar and empty calories, can reduce your immunity), there will be some times during the year when you can benefit from boosting your immune system function – times when you are exposed to a higher amount of infectious agents, such as bacteria and viruses. You know best what times of the year or what conditions can proceed catching a cold or the flu, which means you can do some planning and take preventative measures to strengthen your immunity. *See also Immune System*

| SUPPLEMENT | COMMENTS |
|---|---|
| Beta-carotene | Improves immune function |
| Cat's Claw | Stimulates the immune system |
| CoQ10 | Enhances immune system function |
| Echinacea | Lessens the duration and intensity of colds and flu |
| Ginseng | Boosts immunity |
| Iron | Improves immune system health |
| MSM | Maintains healthy respiratory tract |
| Vitamin A | Improves respiratory system function |
| Vitamin B5 | Strengthens the immune system |
| Vitamin C | Supports overall health |
| Zinc | Supports a healthy immune system |

# Circulation

One of the inside secrets for maintaining optimal health is the promotion of a healthy circulatory system. If you focus your eating, supplement programme and lifestyle around maintaining a healthy circulatory system, everything will start falling into place. You will feel more energetic and you body weight will normalise. There are many nutritritional supplement products that focus on maintaining a healthy circulatory system. Garlic is one of the most popular because of its cholesterol-lowering properties.

| SUPPLEMENT | COMMENTS |
| --- | --- |
| Arginine | Supports circulatory system health |
| Calcium | Normalises blood pressure levels |
| Chitosan | Reduces cholesterol levels |
| Chondroitin Sulphate | Maintains circulatory system health |
| Cod Liver Oil | Promotes a healthy circulatory system |
| Copper | Keeps blood vessels healthy |
| CoQ10 | Lowers blood pressure |
| Evening Primrose Oil | Thins and dilates blood vessels |
| Fibre | Reduces cholesterol |
| Flaxseed Oil | Lowers blood pressure and cholesterol levels |
| Garlic | Protects blood vessels from free radical damage and helps keep blood fluid |

# Circulation (continued)

| SUPPLEMENT | COMMENTS |
|---|---|
| Ginger | Reduces LDL cholesterol levels |
| Ginkgo Biloba | Improves circulation and inhibits blood clotting |
| Ginseng | Decreases blood pressure |
| Glucosamine Sulphate | Strengthens circulatory system health |
| Gotu Kola | Improves circulation and maintains vascular health |
| Grape Seed Extract | Supports circulatory system health |
| Horse Chestnut | Promotes vein structure and function |
| Lutein | Supports circulatory system health |
| Mastika | May decrease blood pressure |
| Omega-3 Fatty Acids | Maintains a healthy circulatory system |
| Red Rice Yeast | Lowers cholesterol levels |
| Vitamin B3 | Increases circulation while reducing blood pressure and cholesterol levels |
| Vitamin E | Reduces cardiovascular disease |
| Vitamin K | Essential for circulatory system health |

# Depression

A depressive disorder is a condition that involves the body, mood and thoughts. It affects the way a person eats and sleeps, the way one feels about oneself, and the way one thinks about things. Depression is not the same as a passing blue mood. It is not a sign of personal weakness or a condition that can be willed or wished away. People with a depressive illness cannot merely "pull themselves together" and get better. Without treatment, symptoms can last for weeks, months or years. Appropriate treatment, however, can help most people who suffer from depression.

| SUPPLEMENT | COMMENTS |
|---|---|
| Black Cohosh | May alleviate depression in menopausal women |
| Kava Kava | Relieves depression and anxiety |
| Magnesium | May ward off depression |
| Royal Jelly | Fights mild depression |
| SAMe | Soothes feelings of depression |
| St John's Wort | Beneficial for mild to moderate depression |
| Vitamin B12 | Used to soothe mild depression |

# Digestion

Among the best-selling prescription and over-the-counter drugs are those aimed at treating stomach and intestinal problems. Peptic ulcers, constipation, diarrhoea, gastroesophageal reflux, gastritis, intestinal gas, and indigestion are among the most common complaints. Health practitioners attribute this pandemic of gastrointestinal disorders to eating too little fibre, too much sugar and processed foods, topped off by an unhealthy dose of chemicals.

There are many nutritional supplements for digestive health. Some are designed for colon health – such as fibre products and probiotics – others are for people with gastrointestinal irritation problems.

| SUPPLEMENT | COMMENTS |
| --- | --- |
| Aloe Vera | Promotes a healthy digestive system |
| Artichoke Extract | Supports digestive health |
| Bee Propolis | Soothes gastrointestinal distress |
| Calcium | Buffers acidity |
| Chloride | Promotes normal digestion |
| Devil's Claw | Aids in digestive health |
| Fibre | Promotes gastrointestinal health |
| Flaxseed Oil | Eases constipation |
| Ginger | Relieves gastrointestinal discomfort |
| Mastika | Eases gastric ulcers |

# Digestion (continued)

| | |
|---|---|
| **Noni** | Traditional treatment for constipation |
| **Probiotics/Prebiotics** | Supports digestive system health |
| **Soy** | Supports digestive health |
| **Vitamin B1** | Aids in digestion |
| **Vitamin B3** | Aids in digestion |
| **Vitamin C** | Acts as a laxative |
| **Wild Yam** | Soothes gastrointestinal distress |

# Energy

Energy – it's what we all want. The fact that most of the world starts off each day with caffeinated beverages such as coffee, tea or guarana stands as a testimony to this desire. Out of all the supplement categories, energy-promoting products represent one of the largest; but it's also one of the most confusing.

Nutritional supplements positioned as energy products fall into several different categories: those that stimulate the nervous system, those that help optimise the metabolism (the way the body turns food into energy), those that contain special concentrated energy sources, and those that actually work at the cellular level to help the body's complex energy-producing biochemical systems function at their best.

| SUPPLEMENT | COMMENTS |
| --- | --- |
| Biotin | Essential in energy production |
| CoQ10 | Improves athletic performance |
| Ginseng | Fights fatigue |
| Guarana | Increases endurance and delays sleep |
| Iron | Prevents fatigue |
| Lecithin | Improves physical performance |
| Magnesium | Improves physical performance |
| Phosphorus | Essential for energy production |
| Royal Jelly | Boosts energy levels |
| Vitamin B3 | Essential for energy production |
| Vitamin B12 | Essential for energy production |

# Healthy Heart

Cardiovascular system problems and diseases are very preventable and treatable with good nutrition, exercise and supplements. Adding supplements can give you an extra advantage in avoiding such problems as congestive heart failure, in which the heart is unable to pump sufficient blood to meet the needs of the body; angina pectoris (discomfort in the chest that results from poor blood supply to the heart); hypertension (due in part to poor circulation); arteriosclerosis (thickening and hardening of the arteries); and high blood lipid levels.

| SUPPLEMENT | COMMENTS |
| --- | --- |
| Avena Sativa fibre | Reduces risk of coronary heart disease |
| Beta-carotene | May reduce risk of cardiovascular disease |
| Calcium | Regulates heartbeat |
| Cod Liver Oil | Promotes a healthy heart |
| CoQ10 | Maintains cardiovascular health |
| Folic Acid | Lowers homocysteine levels |
| Garlic | Improves cardiovascular health |
| Ginkgo Biloba | Increases oxygen supply to the heart |
| Lecithin | Maintains heart health |
| Magnesium | Promotes a healthy heart |
| Noni | May support heart health |

# Healthy Heart *(continued)*

| | |
|---|---|
| **Red Clover** | Supports cardiovascular health |
| **Red Rice Yeast** | Lowers cholesterol |
| **Selenium** | Powerful antioxidant that promotes heart health |
| **Soy** | Promotes cardiovascular wellness |
| **Vitamin B1** | Keeps the heart working properly |
| **Vitamin E** | Promotes cardiovascular wellness |

# Immune System

Maintaining a healthy immune system is essential for your overall well-being. Fortunately, there are steps you can take to easily strengthen your immunity to infectious agents such as bacteria and viruses. Eating a nutritionally balanced diet and taking the proper vitamin and mineral supplements will help to keep your immune system functioning properly. Supplementation with the following nutritional supplements will boost your immune function – supplements are especially helpful for times when you are exposed to a higher amount of infectious agents, such as bacteria and viruses, or times when you may be working too hard or are emotionally stressed. These conditions can contribute to weakening your immune system, leaving you vulnerable to a number of viruses. *See also Colds/Flu*

| SUPPLEMENT | COMMENTS |
|------------|----------|
| Arginine | Stimulates immune system function |
| Beta-carotene | Improves immune function |
| Cat's Claw | Stimulates the immune system |
| Copper | Important to immune system function |
| CoQ10 | Enhances immune system |
| Echinacea | Stimulates immune system |
| Ginseng | Boosts immunity |
| Iron | Improves immune system health |

# Immune System *(continued)*

| | |
|---|---|
| **Lutein** | Improves immune system function |
| **Vitamin A** | Supports immune function |
| **Vitamin B5** | Strengthens the immune system |
| **Vitamin C** | Supports immune function |
| **Vitamin E** | Supports immune function |
| **Zinc** | Supports a healthy immune system |

# Joint Mobility

As we age, our body's capacity to maintain and build connective tissues diminishes. If dietary measures are not taken to provide essential building blocks for these important tissues, degenerative diseases such as arthritis and osteoarthritis may develop. Clinical studies conducted throughout the world have shown that the body will respond positively to nutritional therapy and actually repair degenerated tissues over a course of several weeks to several months.

| SUPPLEMENT | COMMENTS |
|---|---|
| Chondroitin Sulphate | Supports connective tissue health |
| Cod Liver Oil | Maintains joint flexibility |
| Glucosamine | Improves joint repair and function |
| MSM | Promotes joint health |
| Omega-3 Fatty Acids | Maintains joint flexibility |

# Memory

Keeping the brain and nervous system in working order is essential to the health and proper functioning of the entire body. When these degenerate thought, function, and movement are negatively affected. What scientists have determined – as with other degenerative conditions – is that there is a nutrition connection. Inadequate intake of key nutrients is associated with speeding up the breakdown of brain and nervous system tissues, manifesting itself with symptoms of impaired mental function. As with the other nutritionally related degenerative disorders, brain wellness can be maintained, and promotion of brain function can be restored in cases of mental dementias.

| SUPPLEMENT | COMMENTS |
| --- | --- |
| Ginger | Normalises the nervous system |
| Ginkgo Biloba | Sharpens mental acuity |
| Ginseng | Increases cognitive function |
| Gotu Kola | Improves mental function |
| Guarana | Improves alertness |
| Lecithin | Supports brain health |
| Royal Jelly | Increases mental acuity |
| Vitamin B1 | Promotes nervous system health |
| Vitamin B12 | Improves cognitive abilities |
| Zinc | Needed for proper brain function |

# Menopause

The medical term for the usually gradual period of change leading into natural menopause is "perimenopause." The two to three years following the last period are called the "climacteric." During perimenopause, oestrogen production is low and the ovaries stop producing eggs. As oestrogen levels decline, certain signs may appear. The most common sign, the one that doctors sometimes call the hallmark of menopause, is the hot flush. A hot flush is a sudden rush of heat to the neck, face, and possibly other parts of the body that may last from 30 seconds to five minutes. The following supplements may be useful for treating hot flushes and other symptoms of menopause.

| SUPPLEMENT | COMMENTS |
|---|---|
| Agnus Castus | Regulates hormone levels |
| Black Cohosh | Eases menopause symptoms |
| Dong Quai | Eases menopause symptoms |
| Evening Primrose Oil | Regulates hormone levelsalancemenopause |
| Red Clover | Eases menopause symptoms |
| Royal Jelly | Provides support during menopause |
| StarflowerOil | Eases menopause symptoms |
| Wild Yam | Eases menopause symptoms |

# Men's Health/ Prostate Health

As men age, they experience changes in metabolism and hormone levels, causing different types of problems to occur. One problem that many men will experience is declining sexual function. Scientific research has determined that the following supplement ingredients can be effective in promoting male sexual function. However, be patient; it often takes several weeks for improvements to be experienced.

Another situation ageing men often experience is difficulty with their prostate gland. The prostate is a small organ about the size of a walnut. It lies below the bladder and surrounds the urethra (the tube that carries urine from the bladder). The prostate makes a fluid that becomes part of semen (the white fluid that contains sperm). A vast majority of men will experience difficulties with their prostate gland as they age, including enlargement of the prostate, which can cause pain when urinating and other related problems.

| SUPPLEMENT | COMMENTS |
|---|---|
| Avena Sativa | Improves libido |
| Ginkgo Biloba | May treat impotence |
| Lycopene | May reduce the risk of prostate cancer |
| Muira Puama | Treats erectile dysfunction |
| Royal Jelly | May improve sexual function |
| Saw Palmetto | Supports prostate health |
| Selenium | Maintains prostate health and reduces risk of developing prostate cancer |
| Zinc | Necessary for fertility and promotes prostate health |

# PMS

There are several products on the shelves to help nutritionally promote a woman's health. These products consider a woman's unique metabolism and hormonal differences and monthly variations in hormone levels. You will find a number of products that are marketed as reducing the discomfort associated with the menstruation cycle; these products are called PMS supplements. There is a lot of good research backing the use of certain vitamins, minerals and botanicals for reducing the discomfort experienced by some women during their monthly cycles.

| SUPPLEMENT | COMMENTS |
| --- | --- |
| Agnus Castus | Eases PMS discomfort |
| Black Cohosh | Soothes premenstrual pain |
| Dong Quai | Relieves PMS symptoms and regulates hormone levels |
| Evening Primrose Oil | Soothes PMS-related breast pain |
| Kava | Alleviates anxiety and depression |
| Magnesium | Alleviates PMS symptoms |
| Muira Puama | Eases PMS symptoms |
| Valerian | Eases PMS symptoms |
| Wild Yam | Eases PMS symptoms |

# Skin Care

As we age the connective tissues that support the skin breakdown resulting in a loss of tone, wrinkles and poor hydration. Providing your body with a connective tissue nutrient that can help maintain or rebuild the connective tissue matrix is the first step in promoting healthy, beautiful skin. Preventing skin damage from ultraviolet light and free radicals is also important. These supplements may help revitalize your skin.

| SUPPLEMENT | COMMENTS |
|---|---|
| Aloe vera | Has soothing and healing properties |
| Arginine | Promotes wound healing |
| Chondroitin Sulphate | Improves wound healing |
| Cod Liver Oil | Maintains healthy skin |
| Evening Primrose Oil | Maintains healthy skin and used to treat eczema |
| Glucosamine Sulphate | Improves the appearance of skin |
| Gotu Kola | May help alleviate cellulite |
| Grape Seed Extract | Maintains young-looking skin |
| Horse Chestnut | Has anti-swelling properties which may help minimise the appearance of cellulite |
| Iron | Necessary for proper skin tone |
| MSM | Essential for healthy skin |
| Noni | May be useful in treating wounds |

# Skin Care (*continued*)

| | |
|---|---|
| **Omega-3 Fatty Acids** | Maintains healthy skin |
| **Royal Jelly** | Use for younger-looking skin |
| **Starflower Oil** | Relieves eczema-related inflammation |
| **Vitamin A** | Promotes healthy skin |
| **Vitamin B2** | Promotes healthy skin |
| **Vitamin B3** | Promotes healthy skin |
| **Vitamin B6** | Promotes healthy skin |
| **Vitamin C** | Accelerates wound healing and produces collagen |
| **Vitamin E** | Maintains healthy skin. |
| **Zinc** | Enhances wound healing |

# Sleep Problems

It is well known that in our fast-paced, hectic culture many people have dysfunctional sleep patterns. Some of the most widely used drugs are those used to promote restful sleep. Nutritional supplement manufacturers have responded by formulating and marketing a variety of nutritionally based products to help encourage a good night's sleep. If you are having trouble falling and staying asleep, give these supplements a try. They are gentler on your system than drugs and, as a result, may take a few days for improvement to be experienced.

| SUPPLEMENT | COMMENTS |
| --- | --- |
| Kava Kava | Helps promote sleep if related to stress and anxiety |
| St John's Wort | Helps promote sleep if related to depression |
| Valerian | Most effective sleep aid and natural treatment for insomnia |

# Slimming

If you have a weight problem, you must first acknowledge that this can stem from many factors: eating the wrong foods, overeating, inactivity, a reduced metabolism due to ageing, or other lifestyle factors. On the bright side, it doesn't take that much effort to get on the right track toward a healthy weight. The beneficial side effects of committing to a weight loss programme include a trimmer, more attractive body, more energy, reduced stress on joints, and a healthy cardiovascular system.

| SUPPLEMENT | COMMENTS |
|---|---|
| Chitosan | Can function as a weight loss aid |
| Chromium | Can help in weight management |
| CoQ10 | Reduces body fat |
| Fibre | Aids in weight loss by promoting a feeling of fullness |
| Folic Acid | Aids in protein metabolism and utilisation of carbohydrates |
| Garcinia | Promotes weight loss |
| Guarana | Reduces appetite, increases fat metabolism |
| Kelp | Aids metabolism |
| Magnesium | Increases fat loss |
| Royal Jelly | Aids in weight control |
| Vitamin B6 | Metabolises and assimilates fats and protein |
| Vitamin B12 | Promotes a healthy metabolism |

# Stress/ Anxiety

Unfortunately, stress and anxiety are often by-products of our busy, fast-paced lifestyles. While the occasional stressful day may be unavoidable, persistent feelings of stress and anxiety may lead to more serious health problems. If you are feeling stressed or anxious, give the following supplements a try.

| SUPPLEMENT | COMMENTS |
|---|---|
| Calcium | Has a calming effect on the nervous system |
| Dong Quai | Has a mild calming effect |
| Kava Kava | Relieves anxiety and has a calming effect |
| Royal Jelly | Soothes mild anxiety |
| St John's Wort | Alleviates feelings of anxiety and depression |
| Vitamin B1 | Enhances mental attitudes and supports the nervous system |
| Vitamin B2 | Eases stress |
| Vitamin B12 | Eases stress |
| Vitamin BC | Eases stress |

# Section Three:

## Glossary: Understanding Health Terms

This section presents some of the common terms and jargon you will find on supplement labels, in brochures and in the other sections of this guide.

**Adequate Intake:** A value based on observed or experimentally determined estimates of nutrient intake by a group, or groups of healthy people.

**Amino Acids** are a special class of organic molecules that contain nitrogen. They are linked together to form proteins.

**Anaemia** is a condition in which the oxygen-carrying capacity of the blood is reduced. It is the most common symptom of iron-deficiency.

**Antioxidant:** Nutrient that has been found to seek out and neutralise free radicals in the body by preventing oxidation. Prevents cell damage and stimulates the body to recover more quickly from free radical damage.

**Arteriosclerosis:** Hardening and thickening of the arteries.

**Blood Pressure** is the pressure of the blood against the walls of the arteries.

**Botanical:** Refers to ingredients that are of plant origin. A botanical ingredient can be from a whole plant, such as an entire herb or mushroom, or part of a plant, such as seeds, leaves, bark, roots, etc.

**Calorie:** A unit of measurement used to express the energy value of food.

**Capillary:** A tiny blood vessel through which nutrients and waste products travel between the bloodstream and the body's cells.

**Carcinogen:** A substance that is either proven or suspected to cause cancer in humans or laboratory animals.

**Co-enzyme:** An enzyme co-factor, that helps biochemical reactions occur in the body.

**Collagen:** A simple protein that is the chief component of connective tissue.

**Connective Tissue:** Tissue that either supports other tissue or joins tissue to tissue, muscle to bone, or bone to bone. It includes cartilage, bone, tendons, ligaments, blood, bone marrow and lymph.

**Degenerative Illness:** An illness that causes the body to deteriorate. Examples are cancer, cardiovascular disease and arthritis.

**Diuretic:** A substance that increases urination.

**ECRDA:** European Community RDA.

**Enzyme:** One of a group of protein catalysts that initiate or speed chemical reactions in the body without being consumed.

**Essential Nutrient:** A nutrient that the body cannot produce itself or that it cannot produce in sufficient amounts to maintain good health.

**Format (Nutritional supplements):** The major types of supplement formats include

- *Tablets* – start out as a blend of powdered nutrients, which are then pressed by machines into the characteristic round or oval solid form. Tablets are also made in chewable forms. Soluble forms combine convenience with a faster delivery system. Effervescent forms may be preferred for maximum absorption. The term *caplet* is currently being used to describe tablets that are shaped like capsules.

- *Capsules* – are delivery systems that consist of two hollow halves, into which a powder blend is injected. The two halves are then brought together by a machine to form the capsule.

- *Softgels* – were developed to hold liquid nutrient supplements such as lecithin, cod liver oil and vitamin E. They consist of an outer gelatin shell, soft or hard, that is filled with liquid.

- *Powders* – the most common powder formulations are protein powders, diet powders, energy powders, and weight-gain powders. Supplement powders are a convenient way to get high-quality nutrition in the exact amounts you need, when you need it.

- *Liquid supplements* – include protein drinks, carbohydrate drinks, weight-gain drinks, herbal extracts, herbal tinctures, liquid vitamins and minerals, and soluble tablets. Most easily absorbed by the body.

- *Nutrition bars* – currently popular as convenient, better quality nutritional snacks. These scientifically developed snacks are high in healthy carbohydrates and protein, low in fat.

**Free Radicals:** Highly reactive molecules that are known to injure cell membranes, cause defects in the DNA and contribute to the ageing process and a number of degenerative illnesses. Free radicals are by products of normal chemical reactions in the body that involve oxygen.

**High-Density Lipoproteins (HDL):** The good lipoproteins that help prevent cholesterol build up in the arteries.

**Hormones:** Substances produced by the endocrine glands that regulate bodily functions.

**International Unit (IU):** A measure of potency/strength based on an accepted international standard. It is usually used with beta-carotene and vitamins A, D and E.

**Metabolites:** Substances that take part in metabolism. Some are produced in the body as part of the metabolic process, while others are derived from food sources. Some are now also available in supplemental form. Even though the body is able to make many of these substances, taking them can improve the structure or function of the body.

**Minerals:** inorganic nutrients or inorganic-organic complexes that are essential structural components in the body and necessary for many vital metabolic processes, even though they make up only about 4% of the body's weight. Every day the body needs minerals such as calcium in large amounts – about 1,200 milligrams or more – while it needs other minerals, such as chromium, in smaller amounts.

**Osteoporosis:** A condition in which the bones are very porous and can break very easily.

**Oxidation:** A chemical reaction in which an atom or molecule loses electrons or hydrogen atoms.

**RDA (Recommended Daily Allowance):**
Government guidelines of suggested levels of essential nutrients considered adequate to met the nutritional needs of healthy individuals.The RDAs are recommendations for healthy people usually based on the amount needed to reverse nutrient deficiencies. Many RDAs are currently the subject of controversy.

**Standardised:** This term is usually applied to botanical ingredients that are specially prepared to contain an exact amount of one or more of the phytonutrients it contains. By using standardised botanical ingredients, manufacturers can ensure that each product they make will have the same biological activity.

**Sustained Release Tablet:** A tablet that releases its contents slowly and continuously over an extended period of time. Sustained release products offer convenience and improved effectiveness by providing a steady supply of nutrients to your body, all day and night.

**Vitamins:** These are organic compounds that the body needs for the maintenance of good health and for growth. By convention, the name vitamin is reserved for certain nutrients that the body cannot manufacture and are obtained through the food chain.

*Dan Gastelu is a leading American nutritionist who has authored several leading publications within the healthcare industry.*